LEGAL NOTES

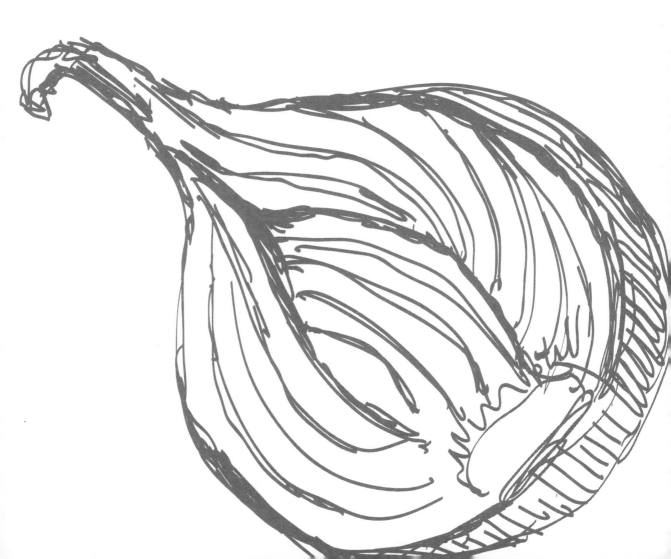

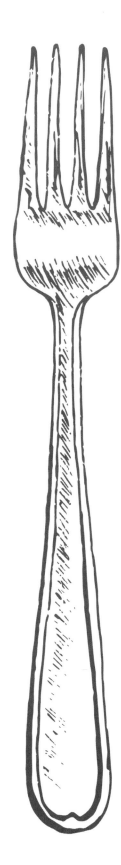

Table of Contents

Risotto

Discover a Delicious Rice Alternative
with Tasty Risotto Recipes

By
BookSumo Press

Published by
http://www.booksumo.com

ENJOY THE RECIPES?
KEEP ON COOKING
WITH 6 MORE FREE COOKBOOKS!

Visit our website and simply enter your email address to join the club and receive your 6 cookbooks.

http://booksumo.com/magnet

https://www.instagram.com/booksumopress/

https://www.facebook.com/booksumo/

Dijon Beef Risotto 48

Seattle Vegetable Risotto 49

Late October Pine Nut Risotto 50

Oyster Mushroom and Barley Risotto 51

Oven Roasted Risotto 52

Sonoma
Orzo Risotto

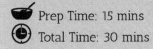 Prep Time: 15 mins

Total Time: 30 mins

Servings per Recipe: 4	
Calories	297.7
Fat	10.1g
Cholesterol	5.5mg
Sodium	358.8mg
Carbohydrates	39.4g
Protein	14.9g

Ingredients

- 2 tsp olive oil
- 2 garlic cloves, chopped
- 1/2 medium onion, chopped
- 1 lb. mushroom, chopped chunks
- 3 tbsp pine nuts
- 1 C. orzo pasta
- 2 C. low sodium chicken broth
- 1/2 tsp ground sage
- 1/4 tsp ground thyme
- 1/4 C. grated parmesan cheese
- 1/2 tsp kosher salt
- ground pepper

Directions

1. Place a large saucepan over medium heat. Heat in it the oil.
2. Cook in it the garlic with onion for 3 min. Stir in the mushrooms with a pinch of salt.
3. Cook them for 4 min. Stir in the sage with thyme and broth. Cook them until they start boiling.
4. Stir in the orzo and lower the heat. Let them cook for 16 min while stirring often.
5. One the time is up, stir in the pine nuts, parmesan cheese, and parsley.
6. Cook them for extra few minutes until the cheese melts. Serve your risotto immediately.
7. Enjoy.

RISOTTO
Mexicana

🥘 Prep Time: 15 mins
🕐 Total Time: 1 hr 15 mins

Servings per Recipe: 4
Calories	495.5
Fat	21.2g
Cholesterol	0.0mg
Sodium	110.5mg
Carbohydrates	63.3g
Protein	16.2g

Ingredients

4 tbsp olive oil
1 onion, chopped
2 garlic cloves, chopped
3/4 C. brown rice
2 1/2 C. vegetable stock
salt and pepper
1 red bell pepper, seeded and chopped
2 celery ribs, sliced

8 oz. cremini mushrooms, sliced
1 (15 oz.) cans red kidney beans
3 tbsp parsley, chopped
3/8 C. cashews

Directions

1. Place a large skillet over medium heat. Heat in it half of the oil.
2. Cook in it the onion for 4 min. Stir in 1 clove of garlic and cook them for 3 min.
3. Stir in the rice and cook them for 2 min. Stir in the stock with a pinch of salt and pepper.
4. Cook them until they start boiling while stirring. Lower the heat and put on the lid.
5. Let the risotto cook for 36 to 42 min.
6. Place pan over medium heat. Heat in it the remaining oil. Cook in it the celery with bell pepper for 6 min.
7. Stir in the mushrooms with the rest of the garlic. Cook them for 4 min while stirring.
8. Add the cooked rice with beans, cashews, and parsley. Cook them for 2 to 3 min while stirring.
9. Adjust the seasoning of your risotto then serve it warm.
10. Enjoy.

Vegan Dessert Risotto

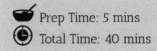

Prep Time: 5 mins
Total Time: 40 mins

Servings per Recipe: 4
Calories   104.8
Fat   0.1g
Cholesterol   0.0mg
Sodium   1.3mg
Carbohydrates   24.5g
Protein   1.2g

Ingredients

7 oz. risotto rice
2 tbsp sugar
1 1/2 C. vanilla-flavored rice milk, warmed
1/2 C. apple juice, unsweetened
1/2 tsp cinnamon
1/8 tsp ground vanilla bean

Additions
fresh fruit etc.

Directions

1. Before you do anything, preheat the oven to 350 F.
2. Get a baking dish and coat it with oil. Stir in it the sugar with rice, milk, and spics.
3. Layover it a piece of foil to cover it then cook it for 26 min in the oven.
4. Once the time is up, top your risotto with your favorite fruit.
5. Cook it for an extra 11 min then serve it warm.
6. Enjoy.

ALLEGHANY
Mushroom Risotto

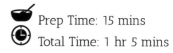

Prep Time: 15 mins
Total Time: 1 hr 5 mins

Servings per Recipe: 6
Calories	305.5
Fat	11.6g
Cholesterol	29.9mg
Sodium	743.2mg
Carbohydrates	36.3g
Protein	12.9g

Ingredients

3 tbsp butter
2 C. mushrooms, sliced
1/2 C. onion, chopped
1 1/4 C. Arborio rice
3 1/2 C. chicken broth

1 C. parmesan cheese, shredded
2 tbsp thyme, chopped

Directions

1. Before you do anything, preheat the oven to 375 F.
2. Place a large ovenproof pan over medium heat. Heat in it the butter.
3. Cook in it the mushrooms with onion for 6 min. Add the rice and cook them for 1 min.
4. Add the broth with a pinch of salt and pepper. Put on the lid and place the pan in the oven for 46 min.
5. Once the time is up, turn off the heat and add the cheese with thyme.
6. Serve your risotto warm.
7. Enjoy.

Arizona
Yellow Risotto

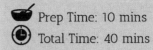

Prep Time: 10 mins
Total Time: 40 mins

Servings per Recipe: 4
Calories	217.8
Fat	21.1g
Cholesterol	68.5mg
Sodium	149.3mg
Carbohydrates	3.3g
Protein	4.8g

Ingredients

2 tbsp butter
1/2 C. sliced mushrooms
1/2 C. chopped onion
2 1/2 C. water
1 (8 oz.) packages Yellow Rice

1/2 C. heavy cream
1/2 C. shredded Monterey jack cheese
1 C. baby spinach leaves

Directions

1. Place a large saucepan over medium heat. Heat in it the butter.
2. Cook in it the mushrooms for 3 min. Add the rice mix with water.
3. Cook them until they start boiling while stirring it often. Lower the heat and put on the lid.
4. Let it cook for 22 min. Once the time is up, add the cream with cheese, a pinch of salt and pepper.
5. Cook them or an extra 4 min. Add the spinach and put on the lid.
6. Turn off the heat and let the risotto rest for 6 min. Serve it immediately.
7. Enjoy.

HOT
Couscous Risotto

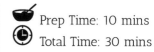

Prep Time: 10 mins
Total Time: 30 mins

Servings per Recipe: 4
Calories	334.3
Fat	7.6g
Cholesterol	0.0mg
Sodium	24.2mg
Carbohydrates	56.6g
Protein	10.1g

Ingredients

2 C. low sodium vegetable broth
2 tbsp olive oil, divided
6 oz. shiitake mushrooms, sliced
1 poblano chile, diced
2 shallots, minced
1 carrot, diced

1 (8 7/8 oz.) boxes Israeli couscous
1/2 peas
3 tbsp chives, chopped
2 tbsp fresh tarragon, chopped

Directions

1. Place a large saucepan over high heat. Heat in it 4 C. of water until they start boiling.
2. Place a pot over medium heat. Heat in it 1 tbsp of oil. Cook in it the poblano with mushrooms for 6 min.
3. Drain them and place them aside. Stir the carrots into the same pot and cook them for 4 min.
4. Stir in the couscous and cook them for an extra 2 min.
5. Lower the heat and stir in 1/4 C. of broth. Cook them while stirring until the couscous absorbs it.
6. Repeat the process with the remaining broth until the couscous absorbs all of it.
7. Stir in the peas with cooked mushrooms and poblano. Cook them for 3 min.
8. Add 3 tbsp of chives with tarragon, a pinch of salt and pepper. Serve your risotto warm.
9. Enjoy.

Josephine's
Risotto

Prep Time: 5 mins
Total Time: 20 mins

Servings per Recipe: 6
Calories   823.9
Fat   44.6g
Cholesterol   117.1mg
Sodium   1043.7mg
Carbohydrates   73.7g
Protein   30.7g

Ingredients

17.5 oz. round short-grain rice
6 C. water
5 oz. butter
2 large onions, minced
10.5 oz. parmesan cheese, grated
5 oz. goat cheese, cubed

9 oz. prosciutto, sliced, optional
1/2 tsp fresh rosemary
1 tbsp olive oil
pepper
salt

Directions

1. Place a large saucepan over medium heat. Heat in it the oil.
2. Cook in it the pepper with onion for 3 min. Stir in the rice and cook them for 1 min.
3. Add the rice and bring them to a rolling boil for 12 min.
4. Stir in the butter with rosemary, parmesan cheese, goat cheese, a pinch of salt and pepper.
5. Garnish your risotto with prosciutto then serve it.
6. Enjoy.

LEMON
Pepper Cookout Risotto

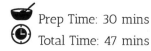

Prep Time: 30 mins
Total Time: 47 mins

Servings per Recipe: 4
Calories	626.0
Fat	29.0g
Cholesterol	69.4mg
Sodium	1491.5mg
Carbohydrates	61.3g
Protein	27.9g

Ingredients

Marinade
1/4 C. olive oil
1 tsp sea salt
1/4 tsp red pepper flakes
1/4 tsp dried rosemary
1/2 tsp oregano
1/4 tsp lemon pepper
2 large boneless skinless chicken breasts
Rice
3 quarts water
1 1/2 C. Arborio rice
1 tsp salt
1 C. mozzarella cheese, shredded
1/4 C. parmesan cheese, shredded
1 tbsp unsalted butter
2 C. baby arugula
1 C. mushroom, sliced
1 tbsp olive oil
black pepper

Directions

1. Get a large mixing bowl: Stir in it all the marinade ingredients.
2. Stir in the chicken breasts and poke them all over with a fork. Let them sit for 35 min.
3. Before you do anything, preheat the grill and grease it.
4. Drain the chicken breasts and grill them for 6 to 8 min on each side.
5. Cover them with a piece of foil and place them aside.
6. Place a large pot over medium heat. Bring in it the water to a boil.
7. Cook in it the rice with a pinch of salt until they start boiling. Keep it boiling for 16 to 18 min while stirring.
8. Place a skillet over medium heat. Heat in it the olive oil. Cook in it the mushroom for 5 min.
9. Strain the rice and add it the same skillet with cheese, butter, and arugula. Cook them until the cheese melts. Top your risotto with grilled chicken then serve them warm. Enjoy.

Yam Risotto

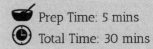 Prep Time: 5 mins

Total Time: 30 mins

Servings per Recipe: 4
Calories	429.4
Fat	21.9g
Cholesterol	41.5mg
Sodium	292.1mg
Carbohydrates	48.8g
Protein	9.6g

Ingredients

4 tbsp butter
2 tbsp minced shallots
1 medium sweet potato, cubed
1/3 C. chopped pecans
2 - 3 C. vegetable broth
1 C. Arborio rice

salt & ground black pepper
1/2 C. grated parmesan cheese
1 tbsp chopped green onion tops

Directions

1. Place a large saucepan over medium heat. Bring in it the broth to a boil.
2. Place a pot over medium heat. Heat in it the butter. Cook in it the pecans with shallot for 4 min.
3. Stir in the rice and cook them for 2 min. Add the sweet potato with 3/4 C. of boiling broth.
4. Let them cook until the rice absorbs the broth while stirring.
5. Repeat the process with the remaining broth until the rice absorbs all of it and becomes creamy.
6. Add the green onion with cheese, a pinch of salt and pepper. Serve your risotto warm.
7. Enjoy.

FRUIT
Risotto

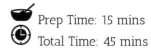 Prep Time: 15 mins
Total Time: 45 mins

Servings per Recipe: 4
Calories   289.7
Fat   7.3g
Cholesterol   16.3mg
Sodium   443.5mg
Carbohydrates   51.2g
Protein   5.7g

Ingredients

2 tbsp butter
3 garlic cloves, roasted
1 small onion, diced
3/4 C. Arborio rice
2 C. chicken broth

3/4 C. dried sweetened cranberries
1 tbsp parmesan cheese

Directions

1. Before you do anything, preheat the oven to 400 F.
2. Coat a baking dish with some oil. Place it aside.
3. Place a pot over medium heat. Heat in it the butter. Cook in it the onion with garlic for 2 min.
4. Stir in the rice and cook them for 1 min. Stir in the broth with cranberries.
5. Cook them until they start boiling. Spoon the mixture into the greased pan.
6. Place it in the oven and let it cook for 26 min. Add the cheese then serve it.
7. Enjoy.

Twin City
Suburb Risotto

🍲 Prep Time: 5 mins
🕐 Total Time: 45 mins

Servings per Recipe: 4
Calories	823.7
Fat	42.6g
Cholesterol	74.9mg
Sodium	1688.4mg
Carbohydrates	69.6g
Protein	39.4g

Ingredients

2 tbsp extra virgin olive oil
1 lb. Italian sausage, sweet, casings removed
1 onion, large, sliced
1 garlic clove, large, minced
1 1/2 C. orzo pasta
2 C. chicken stock
salt and pepper

1 C. marinated artichoke drained and quartered
1 C. frozen baby peas
3 tbsp chives, snipped
6 tbsp parmesan cheese, grated
parmesan cheese

Directions

1. Place a large pan over medium heat. Heat in it the oil.
2. Cook in it the sausage for 6 min. Drain it and place it aside.
3. Lower the heat and stir the garlic with onion into the same pan.
4. Put on the lid and let them cook for 5 min. Stir in the orzo and let them cook for 2 min.
5. Stir in 2 C. of water with stock, a pinch of salt and pepper.
6. Cook them for 16 min while stirring often until the risotto becomes creamy.
7. Stir in the sausage, artichokes, peas, chives, and parmesan. Cook them for 5 min.
8. Serve your risotto hot.
9. Enjoy.

RISOTTO
Kerala Style

Prep Time: 10 mins
Total Time: 40 mins

Servings per Recipe: 8
Calories	386.3
Fat	9.5g
Cholesterol	17.0mg
Sodium	248.9mg
Carbohydrates	63.8g
Protein	11.9g

Ingredients

1 tbsp grapeseed oil
1 tbsp sesame oil
15 curry leaves, washed, dried, and julienned
2 green chilies, washed, dried, and sliced
2 tbsp cumin seeds
1 tbsp black mustard seeds
2 onions, diced

8 oz. mushrooms, diced
4 carrots, peeled and grated
2 C. jasmine rice, uncooked
4 C. of warm milk
15 oz. chickpeas, canned
salt

Directions

1. Place a large saucepan over medium heat. Stir in it the grapeseed oil, sesame oil, curry leaves and green chilies.
2. Cook them for 1 min. Stir in the cumin seeds and mustard seeds. Cook them for an extra 2 min.
3. Stir in the onions, mushrooms, and carrots. Cook them for 4 min.
4. Stir in the rice with a pinch of salt and pepper. Cook them for 3 min while stirring.
5. Add the milk gradually while stirring until the rice becomes creamy.
6. Stir in the chickpeas with a pinch of salt and pepper.
7. Garnish your risotto with some cilantro, chopped fresh onions, tomatoes, cucumber, yogurt and raita then serve it.
8. Enjoy.

Sweet
Bavarian Risotto

Prep Time: 2 mins
Total Time: 12 mins

Servings per Recipe: 4
Calories	396.5
Fat	20.0g
Cholesterol	44.1mg
Sodium	41.0mg
Carbohydrates	52.7g
Protein	5.1g

Ingredients

1 C. White Rice, uncooked
1 C. milk
1/3 C. sugar
2 tbsp unsalted butter

1/4 C. heavy cream
1/2 C. semi-sweet chocolate chips

Directions

1. Place a large saucepan over medium heat. Stir in the sugar with milk, rice and a pinch of salt.
2. Cook them until they start boiling. Turn off the heat and put on the lid.
3. Let the risotto rest for 6 min. Add the cream with chocolate chips and butter.
4. Adjust the seasoning of your risotto then serve it.
5. Enjoy.

HOT
Tuna Risotto

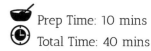 Prep Time: 10 mins

Total Time: 40 mins

Servings per Recipe: 4
Calories	463.3
Fat	6.1g
Cholesterol	46.2mg
Sodium	730.6mg
Carbohydrates	64.9g
Protein	33.7g

Ingredients

1 1/4 C. Arborio rice
4 C. chicken stock
13 oz. canned tuna, slices in spring water
1 onion, chopped
1/4 C. stock, extra
1 - 2 tsp chili, minced
1 tbsp lemon juice

1 lemon, zest of
3/4 C. frozen peas
1 tbsp of oil
parmesan cheese

Directions

1. Place a large deep pan over medium heat. Heat in it the oil.
2. Cook in it the onion with chili and rice for 2 min. Stir 1 C. of stock and heat them until they start boiling.
3. Lower the heat and let them cook while stirring often until the rice absorbs it.
4. Repeat the process with the remaining broth until the risotto becomes creamy.
5. Stir in the peas, tuna and lemon juice and zest. Heat them for 2 min. Serve it warm.
6. Enjoy.

Parmesan
Pesto Risotto

Prep Time: 10 mins
Total Time: 40 mins

Servings per Recipe: 2
Calories   363.5
Fat   10.0g
Cholesterol   24.2mg
Sodium   482.3mg
Carbohydrates   55.2g
Protein   14.0g

Ingredients

1 C. risotto rice (Arborio)
2 1/2 C. chicken stock
1 tbsp butter
1 red bell pepper, chopped
1 onion, chopped
1 tomatoes, chopped
1/2 zucchini, chopped
1/3 C. peas

1/2 C. mushroom, sliced
2 - 3 tbsp pesto sauce, see appendix
parmesan cheese, grated
salt and pepper

Directions

1. Place a pot deep pan over medium heat. Heat in it the butter. Cook in it the onion for 2 min.
2. Stir in the pepper and cook them for 2 min. Lower the heat and stir in the rice.
3. Cook them for 1 min. Stir in 1/4 C. of bouillon and cook them until the rice absorbs it while stirring.
4. Stir in the tomato with zucchini. Cook them for 22 min while stirring adding more broth when needed.
5. Stir in the mushrooms with a pinch of salt and pepper. Cook them for 5 min while stirring.
6. Stir in the peas with any bouillon left. Season them with a pinch of salt and pepper.
7. Serve your risotto warm with toppings of your choice.
8. Enjoy.

SLOW COOKER
Risotto

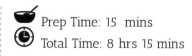

Prep Time: 15 mins
Total Time: 8 hrs 15 mins

Servings per Recipe: 4

Calories	359.4
Fat	2.6g
Cholesterol	0.0mg
Sodium	44.3mg
Carbohydrates	77.2g
Protein	9.0g

Ingredients

1/2 tbsp olive oil
2 - 2 1/2 onions, chopped
1 tsp minced garlic
1/2 tsp dried rosemary
1 1/2 C. pearl barley

3 C. vegetable stock
2 sweet potatoes, peeled and chopped

Directions

1. Place a large pan over medium heat. Heat in it the oil.
2. Cook in it the onion for 2 min. Stir in the garlic with rosemary. Cook them for 1 min.
3. add the barley and cook them for 2 min. Stir in the stock and cook them until they start boiling.
4. Spoon the mixture to a stockpot. Add the sweet potato and put on the lid.
5. Let them cook for 7 to 8 h on low.
6. Adjust the seasoning of your risotto then serve it warm.
7. Enjoy.

Simple
Long Grain Risotto

Prep Time: 15 mins
Total Time: 35 mins

Servings per Recipe: 4
Calories   153.0
Fat   2.1g
Cholesterol   5.8mg
Sodium   677.5mg
Carbohydrates   27.5g
Protein   5.2g

Ingredients

1/3 C. onion, chopped
1 tbsp garlic, minced
2/3 C. long grain rice
2 C. water
2 tsp instant chicken bouillon granules

1/4 tsp black pepper, ground
1/4 C. parmesan cheese, grated

Directions

1. Place a large saucepan over medium heat. Heat in it the butter.
2. Cook in it the onion with garlic for 3 min. Stir in the rice and cook them for 1 min.
3. Add the water with bouillon granules. Cook them until they start boiling.
4. Lower the heat and put on the lid. Let them cook for 22 to 26 min.
5. Turn off the heat and stir in the cheese until the risotto becomes creamy.
6. Serve it immediately.
7. Enjoy.

RISOTTO
Alaska

Prep Time: 10 mins
Total Time: 30 mins

Servings per Recipe: 2
Calories	580.6
Fat	20.1g
Cholesterol	220.4mg
Sodium	494.0mg
Carbohydrates	21.7g
Protein	73.1g

Ingredients

2 fresh salmon fillets
3 oz. shrimp
1 vegetable stock cube
5 oz. risotto rice
1 pint boiling water
2 bay leaves
2 tbsp crème fraiche
2 tsp dried dill

1 tsp dried herbs
lemon juice
lemon zest
olive oil
salt and pepper

Directions

1. Place a large deep pan over medium heat. Heat in it the oil.
2. Cook in it the dry herbs with bay leaf, and rice. Cook them for 6 min.
3. Stir in 1/3 C. of stock and cook them for 6 min while stirring.
4. Repeat the process with the remaining stock until the all of it is absorbed.
5. Place a skillet of over medium heat: Stir in 1 tbsp olive oil, lemon zest, crème fraiche and dill.
6. Heat them for 2 min. Add the salmon fillets and cook them for 4 to 6 min on each side.
7. Flake it and place it aside.
8. Stir the lemon juice with shrimp, a pinch of salt and pepper into the risotto.
9. Cook them for 6 min. Discard the bay leaves and stir in the salmon. Serve it immediately.
10. Enjoy.

Summer
Celery Risotto

Prep Time: 15 mins
Total Time: 45 mins

Servings per Recipe: 4
Calories   363.5
Fat   10.0g
Cholesterol   24.2mg
Sodium   482.3mg
Carbohydrates   55.2g
Protein   14.0g

Ingredients

2 tbsp butter
3 shallots, chopped
2 sticks celery, chopped
1 tbsp extra virgin olive oil
2 C. Arborio rice
1 1/2-2 liters vegetable stock
1 lemon, zest
1/4 C. lemon juice, squeezed

1 tsp dried rosemary
6 tbsp parmesan cheese, grated
1/3 C. heavy cream
2 tbsp butter
salt and pepper

Directions

1. Get a mixing bowl: Stir in it the lemon juice, cream, and parmesan.
2. Place a large pan over medium heat. Heat in it the oil with 2 tbsp of butter.
3. Cook in it the celery with shallot for 4 min. Stir in the rice and cook them for 1 min.
4. Stir in 1 C. of stock. Cook them until the rice absorbs it.
5. Repeat the process with the remaining broth until the rice is done.
6. Stir in the lemon zest and rosemary.
7. Remove the pan from the heat and add to it the butter with a pinch of salt and pepper.
8. Serve your risotto immediately.
9. Enjoy.

HOT
Salami Risotto

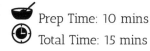

Prep Time: 10 mins
Total Time: 15 mins

Servings per Recipe: 4
Calories   510.0
Fat   18.4g
Cholesterol   28.7mg
Sodium   704.3mg
Carbohydrates   71.3g
Protein   14.7g

Ingredients

2 tbsp olive oil
1 large onion, chopped
1 1/2 C. Arborio rice
15 oz. tomatoes
3 C. water
3.5 oz. spicy salami, chopped
1/4 C. sun-dried tomato, drained and sliced

1/2 C. black olives, seeded and sliced
1 tsp dried chili pepper flakes
1/2 C. grated parmesan cheese

Directions

1. Place a large skillet over medium heat. Heat in it the oil.
2. Cook in it the onion for 3 min. Stir in the rice and cook them for 2 min.
3. Stir in the tomatoes with water. Cook them until they start boiling.
4. Lower the heat and put on the lid. Cook them for 16 min.
5. Turn off the heat and let the risotto rest for 12 min.
6. Add the chili flakes with olives, dried tomato, cheese, and salami. Serve it warm.
7. Enjoy.

Spanish
Risotto con Azafran

Prep Time: 20 mins

Total Time: 40 mins

Servings per Recipe: 4
Calories	446.7
Fat	9.7g
Cholesterol	96.2mg
Sodium	707.3mg
Carbohydrates	65.7g
Protein	23.4g

Ingredients

8 oz. peas
4 oz. zucchini, sliced
2 tbsp olive oil
1 onion, chopped
1/2 tsp saffron thread
4 oz. Arborio rice
4 cloves garlic, crushed
8 oz. button mushrooms, sliced

1 lemon, juice and rind
3 C. fish stock
10.5 oz. cooked prawns, peeled, tails intact
3 tbsp chopped flat leaf parsley

Directions

1. Bring a large saucepan of water to a boil. Cook in it the zucchini with peas for 2 min.
2. Drain them, dip them in cold water and drain them again.
3. Place a large skillet over medium heat. Heat in it the oil.
4. Cook in it the onion with saffron for 3 min. Stir in the rice, garlic, and mushrooms.
5. Cook them for 3 min. Stir in the lemon rind with 1/3 of the stock while stirring.
6. Cook them until the rice absorbs it. Repeat the process with the remaining stock until the rice becomes creamy.
7. Stir in the prawns, blanched vegetables, and lemon juice. Season them with a pinch of salt and pepper.
8. Cook them for 2 min. Add the parsley and serve it warm.
9. Enjoy.

ZUCCHINI
Risotto

Prep Time: 10 mins
Total Time: 25 mins

Servings per Recipe: 4

Calories	292.9
Fat	9.0g
Cholesterol	15.8mg
Sodium	199.8mg
Carbohydrates	40.8g
Protein	13.1g

Ingredients

1 small zucchini, chopped
1 shallot, chopped
1 tbsp olive oil
2 garlic cloves, minced
1 C. orzo pasta
2 C. vegetable broth
1 C. milk
6 oz. spinach

2 tomatoes, chopped
1/4 C. basil
1/3 C. parmesan cheese
1/4 tsp salt and pepper

Directions

1. Place a pot over medium heat. Heat in it the oil. Cook in it the zucchini with shallot for 3 min.
2. Stir in the garlic and cook them for 2 min. Stir in the orzo, broth, and milk.
3. Cook them until they start boiling. Lower the heat and let it cook for 12 to 16 min while stirring.
4. Once the time is up, add the basil with tomato, spinach, a pinch of salt and pepper.
5. Cook them for 3 min. Turn off the heat and add the cheese. Serve your risotto right away.
6. Enjoy.

Moroccan
Lamb Risotto

Prep Time: 10 mins
Total Time: 1 hr 20 mins

Servings per Recipe: 6
Calories	231.0
Fat	13.1g
Cholesterol	10.1mg
Sodium	44.0mg
Carbohydrates	26.1g
Protein	3.7g

Ingredients

Lamb Sausage
6 large fresh lamb sausages
water, for boiling
1 tbsp canola oil
fresh rosemary sprig
Risotto
4 large Yukon gold potatoes, diced cubes
salt
3 tbsp extra-virgin olive oil

1 large shallot, minced
3 C. stock
6 large fresh mushrooms, sliced
kosher salt & ground black pepper
1 C. loosely packed grated Parmigiano
2 - 4 tbsp butter
baby arugula

Directions

1. To prepare the sausages:
2. Bring a large salted saucepan of water to a boil. Cook in it the sausages for 7 min.
3. Drain it and place it aside.
4. Place a skillet over medium heat. Heat in it the oil. Cook in it the rosemary needles for 30 sec.
5. Stir in the sausages and cook them for 6 in. Drain them and place them aside.
6. To prepare the risotto:
7. Bring a large salted pot of water to a boil. Cook in it the potatoes for 6 min. Drain them.
8. Place a pot over medium heat. Heat in it the oil. Cook in it the shallot with potatoes, a pinch of salt and pepper for 3 min.
9. Stir in a ladle of stock and cook them until it is absorbed. Repeat the process with the remaining stock until all of it is absorbed.
10. Place a skillet over medium heat. Heat in it a drizzle of olive oil.
11. Cook in it the mushrooms for 8 min. Stir them into the risotto with cheese, butter, a pinch of salt and pepper. Spoon the sausage on top then serve it warm Enjoy.

MEDITERRANEAN
Veal Risotto

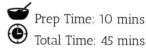

Prep Time: 10 mins
Total Time: 45 mins

Servings per Recipe: 4
Calories	1010.1
Fat	51.0g
Cholesterol	119.9mg
Sodium	1144.0mg
Carbohydrates	115.0g
Protein	24.8g

Ingredients

Risotto
4 C. chicken stock
1 onion, chopped
1 tbsp olive oil
2 C. Arborio rice
1/4 C. butter
1 C. feta cheese, grated
1 C. feta cheese, cubed
4 C. spinach
1 lemon, juice and zest
Shrimp
1 tbsp canola oil
12 large shrimp, cleaned and deveined,
tail intact
2 tbsp ouzo
2 tbsp butter
sea salt & ground black pepper
1/4 C. fresh parsley, chopped

Stock
8 meaty veal bones, chopped
3 tbsp canola oil
sea salt & ground black pepper
1 tbsp tomato paste
1 head garlic
6 carrots
2 onions
4 stalks celery
2 large leeks
4 sprigs fresh thyme
4 sprigs fresh rosemary
4 large sprigs fresh flat-leaf parsley
17 C. water

Directions

1. To prepare the stock:
2. Before you do anything, preheat the oven to 450 F.
3. Place a meat on in a roasting dish. Top them with the bones, a drizzle of olive oil, salt, and pepper.
4. Place the pan in the oven and let them cook for 30 min. Stir them and cook them for an extra 30 min.
5. Once the time is up, stir in the tomato paste with veggies. Cook them for another 60 min.

6. Transfer the mixture to a large pot. Stir in the water with herbs, a pinch of salt and pepper.
7. Stir 1/2 C. of water into the roasting pan, stir it and add it to the pot.
8. Cook them until they start boiling. Lower the heat and put on the lid.
9. Let the stock cook for 8 h while adding water if needed and skimming the fat every once in a while.
10. Once the time is up, strain the stock and discard the fat. Place it aside to cool down completely.
11. Pour it into airtight containers and freeze them until ready to use.
12. To prepare the risotto:
13. Place a pot over medium heat. Heat in it the oil.
14. Cook in it the onion for 4 min. Stir in the rice and cook them for 1 min.
15. Stir in 3/4 C. of broth and cook them while stirring until the rice absorbs it.
16. Repeat the process with the remaining stock while stirring until the risotto becomes creamy over low heat.
17. Once the time is up, stir in the cheeses with butter. Cook them for 1 min.
18. Stir in the spinach and the lemon juice. Adjust the seasoning of your risotto and place it aside.
19. To prepare the shrimp:
20. Place a large pan over medium heat. Heat in it the oil.
21. Cook in it the shrimp for 3 to 4 min. Season it with a pinch of salt and pepper.
22. Arrange it over the risotto then serve it warm.
23. Enjoy.

NEW ENGLAND
Ginger Risotto

🥣 Prep Time: 20 mins
🕐 Total Time: 25 mins

Servings per Recipe: 4
Calories	367.5
Fat	5.5g
Cholesterol	234.2mg
Sodium	2230.7mg
Carbohydrates	55.0g
Protein	21.1g

Ingredients

4 C. hot cooked rice
7 oz. canned crabmeat
4 eggs
1 scallion
4 C. dashi
2 tbsp mirin
2 tsp salt
3 tbsp light soy sauce

1 tbsp fresh ginger juice
1/4 sheet nori

Directions

1. Remove the white tendons from the crab meat. Use a fork to flake them.
2. Place a large saucepan over medium heat. Stir in it the dashi with spices.
3. Cook them until they start boiling. Stir in the crabmeat with rice. Bring them to another boil.
4. Lower the heat and let them cook for 3 to 4 min. Stir in the ginger juice with beaten eggs while stirring.
5. Cook them for 1 to 2 min. Turn off the heat and put on the lid.
6. Spoon the risotto into the serving bowl. Top them with nori and serve them.
7. Enjoy.

Oriental
Risotto

Prep Time: 10 mins
Total Time: 50 mins

Servings per Recipe: 6
Calories   370.8
Fat   9.3g
Cholesterol   46.7mg
Sodium   129.6mg
Carbohydrates   53.4g
Protein   17.6g

Ingredients

2 - 3 leeks, sliced and divided
4 C. almond breeze milk
1 - 2 tbsp Thai red curry paste, see appendix
1 tbsp dried unsweetened coconut
2 boneless skinless chicken breasts, cubed
1 tsp coconut oil
1 garlic clove, minced

2 red sliced bell peppers
1 1/2 C. Arborio rice
1 bunch chopped basil

Directions

1. Place a large saucepan over high heat. Stir in it half of the leeks with Almond Breeze Unsweetened Original, Thai paste and dried coconut.
2. Cook them until they start boiling. Stir in the chicken breasts and cook them for 7 to 9 min.
3. Place a large saucepan over medium heat. Heat in it the oil.
4. Cook in it the remaining leeks with peppers and garlic for 6 min.
5. Add the rice and cook them for 2 min. Stir in the chicken mixture. Lower the heat and put on the lid.
6. Cook the risotto for 14 to 16 min while stirring from time to time.
7. Adjust the seasoning of your risotto then serve it warm.
8. Enjoy.

ENGLISH
Tuna Risotto

Prep Time: 10 mins
Total Time: 50 mins

Servings per Recipe: 4
Calories	186.3
Fat	8.4g
Cholesterol	24.2mg
Sodium	576.8mg
Carbohydrates	18.7g
Protein	8.6g

Ingredients

Tuna
4 tuna steaks
1 tbsp Worcestershire sauce
1 tsp salt and pepper
1 tbsp lemon juice
Risotto
1 C. risotto rice
2 C. chicken broth

2 C. water
1 onion, diced
1 garlic clove, crushed
1 tbsp butter
3/4 C. shredded mozzarella cheese
2 tbsp lemon juice

Directions

1. To prepare the risotto:
2. Place a large skillet over medium heat. Heat in it the butter.
3. Cook in it the onion for 3 min. Stir in the rice and cook them for 1 min. Lower the heat and stir in ½ C. broth and 2 tbsp lemon juice until the rice absorbs it. Repeat the process with the remaining broth and water until all of it is absorbed while stirring.
4. Cook them until the risotto is creamy.
5. To prepare the tuna:
6. Get a mixing bowl: Whisk in it the Worcestershire sauce and lemon juice. Coat the tuna steaks with the mixture. Season them with a pinch of salt and pepper.
7. Place a large skillet over medium heat. Heat in it the oil.
8. Cook in it the steaks for 2 to 3 min on each side. Serve them warm with the risotto.
9. Enjoy.

Mushroom Florets Risotto

🥣 Prep Time: 15 mins

🕐 Total Time: 1 hr

Servings per Recipe: 4

Calories	238.3
Fat	15.4g
Cholesterol	24.9mg
Sodium	628.5mg
Carbohydrates	12.3g
Protein	15.0g

Ingredients

1 onion, sliced

4 oz. mushrooms, sliced

2 tbsp extra virgin olive oil, divided

1 cauliflower head, riced

1/4 C. flat leaf parsley, chopped

1 tbsp fresh rosemary, chopped

4 oz. parmesan cheese, grated

1 C. almond milk

1/4 tsp salt

1/4 tsp pepper

Directions

1. Before you do anything, preheat the oven to 350 F.
2. Place a large skillet over medium heat. Heat in it 1 tbsp of EVOO.
3. Cook in it the onion for 3 min. Turn off the heat.
4. Get a mixing bowl: Toss in it the herbs with cauliflower and Evoo. Pour the mixture into a baking sheet.
5. Cook them in the oven for 32 min.
6. In the meantime, place a pan over medium heat.
7. Stir in it the baked cauliflower with onion, mushroom, cheese, milk, a pinch of salt and pepper.
8. Cook them until they start boiling. Lower the heat and let them cook for 6 min. Serve it warm.
9. Enjoy.

HOLIDAY
Risotto

🍲 Prep Time: 20 mins
🕐 Total Time: 1 hr

Servings per Recipe: 4
Calories   506.1
Fat   15.1g
Cholesterol   5.5mg
Sodium   109.7mg
Carbohydrates   83.6g
Protein   12.1g

Ingredients

3 lb. pumpkin, peeled and diced
2 tbsp oil
4 C. of boiling vegetable stock
1 onion, diced
2 garlic cloves, crushed
1 1/2 C. Arborio rice
1 1/2 C. baby spinach leaves
1/4 C. parmesan cheese

1/4 C. pine nuts, toasted
extra grated parmesan cheese

Directions

1. Before you do anything, preheat the oven to 400 F.
2. Put the pumpkin in a baking pan. Cook it in the oven for 22 min.
3. Place a large saucepan over medium heat. Heat in it the oil.
4. Cook in it the garlic with onion for 6 min. Add the rice and cook them for 1 min.
5. Stir 1 C. of boiling stock. Cook them until the rice absorbs while stirring.
6. Repeat the process with the remaining stock until all of it is absorbed.
7. Add the cheese with pine nuts, pumpkin, spinach, a pinch of salt and pepper. Serve it warm.
8. Enjoy.

September's
Quinoa Risotto

Prep Time: 15 mins
Total Time: 30 mins

Servings per Recipe: 4
Calories	196.1
Fat	6.1g
Cholesterol	0.0mg
Sodium	584.7mg
Carbohydrates	29.3g
Protein	6.3g

Ingredients

1 tbsp olive oil
1 C. quinoa
1/2 onion, chopped
1 garlic clove, chopped
1 tsp ginger, chopped
2 C. vegetable broth
2 tsp curry powder
3 C. vegetables, diced

1 tsp salt
1 dash cayenne

Directions

1. Place a large skillet over medium heat. Heat in it the oil.
2. Cook in it the onions, garlic, and ginger for 3 min. Stir in the quinoa and cook them for 2 min.
3. Stir in the broth and cook them until they start boiling. Lower the heat and add the curry powder.
4. Put on the lid and let them cook for 6 min. Stir in the veggies and cook them until all the broth is absorbed.
5. Adjust the seasoning of your risotto then serve it warm.
6. Enjoy.

AUGUST'S
Quinoa Risotto

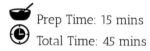 Prep Time: 15 mins

Total Time: 45 mins

Servings per Recipe: 4
Calories	636.7
Fat	30.9g
Cholesterol	41.6mg
Sodium	404.8mg
Carbohydrates	64.2g
Protein	26.8g

Ingredients

4 tbsp olive oil
1 onion, chopped
3 garlic cloves, minced
10 -15 button mushrooms, sliced
1 summer squash, sliced
2 C. quinoa
3 C. vegetable broth
1 C. milk

1 C. mozzarella cheese
1/2 C. parmesan cheese
salt and pepper

Directions

1. Place a large saucepan over medium heat. Heat in it the oil.
2. Cook in it the onion with garlic for 3 min. Stir in the mushrooms and cook them for 4 min.
3. Stir in the zucchini and cook them for 2 to 3 min. Stir in the quinoa and cook them for 1 min.
4. Stir in 1 C. of broth and cook them until the quinoa absorbs it.
5. Repeat the process with the remaining broth. Stir in the milk and cook the risotto until it becomes creamy.
6. Stir in the cheese with a pinch of salt and pepper. Heat it until it melts. Serve it warm.
7. Enjoy.

Gilroy
Garlic Risotto

🥣 Prep Time: 10 mins
🕐 Total Time: 40 mins

Servings per Recipe: 4
Calories   527.5
Fat   12.2g
Cholesterol   14.8mg
Sodium   772.5mg
Carbohydrates   90.7g
Protein   12.8g

Ingredients

2 C. Arborio rice
1 onion
2 vegetable bouillon cubes, dissolved in 1 ltr. hot water
1 bulb of garlic, minced
2 tbsp soy sauce
1 tsp chili flakes
1 tbsp basil

1 C. bell pepper
1/2 C. cheddar cheese
2/3 C. stewed tomatoes
2 tbsp olive oil
salt and pepper

Directions

1. Place a large saucepan over medium heat. Heat in it the oil. Cook in it the onion with garlic for 6 min.
2. Stir in the peppers and cook them for 3 min. Stir in the rice and cook them or 1 min.
3. Stir in a ladle of stock with the stewed tomatoes. Cook them while stirring the rice absorbs it.
4. Stir in the soy sauce, chili flakes, and basil.
5. Add the remaining stock gradually while stirring until the rice absorbs it all.
6. Stir into the cheese with a pinch of salt and pepper. Serve your risotto warm.
7. Enjoy.

5-INGREDIENT
Seafood Risotto

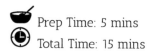 Prep Time: 5 mins
Total Time: 15 mins

Servings per Recipe: 2
Calories	342.5
Fat	22.7g
Cholesterol	281.4mg
Sodium	365.7mg
Carbohydrates	2.5g
Protein	30.9g

Ingredients

10.5 oz. approx. king prawns, defrosted
2 oz. butter
2 - 4 large garlic cloves, crushed
1 package of ready cooked mushroom

rice
salt and pepper

Directions

1. Place a skillet over medium heat. Heat in it the butter. Cook in it the garlic with prawns for 3 min.
2. Prepare the mushroom rice by following the instructions on the package.
3. Serve it warm with prawns.
4. Enjoy.

Risotto
with Scallops

🍲 Prep Time: 5 mins
🕐 Total Time: 35 mins

Servings per Recipe: 4
Calories   537.7
Fat   11.4g
Cholesterol   27.2mg
Sodium   483.1mg
Carbohydrates   84.6g
Protein   21.5g

Ingredients

1 tbsp oil
cracked black pepper and sea salt
1 lb. scallops
5 1/2 C. of boiling vegetable stock
2 tbsp oil
2 C. Arborio rice

2 tsp lemon rind, grated
6 1/2 oz. baby spinach leaves
cracked black pepper and sea salt
parmesan cheese, shavings

Directions

1. Place a large saucepan over medium heat. Heat in it the oil.
2. Cook in it the rice for 1 min. Stir in the stock gradually while stirring until the rice absorbs it all.
3. Season it with a pinch of salt and pepper. Add the spinach with lemon rind.
4. Place a skillet over high heat. Season the scallops with a pinch of salt and pepper.
5. Sear them for 25 to 35 sec on each side. Spoon them over the risotto and serve them warm.
6. Enjoy.

KATHY'S
Potluck Risotto

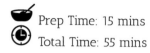 Prep Time: 15 mins

Total Time: 55 mins

Servings per Recipe: 4

Calories	1020.7
Fat	26.7g
Cholesterol	77.8mg
Sodium	1896.9mg
Carbohydrates	147.1g
Protein	42.8g

Ingredients

10.5 oz. boneless skinless chicken breasts, diced
12 oz. rice
2 oz. onions, minced
4 tbsp olive oil
7 oz. plum tomatoes, peeled, seeded and diced
24.5 oz. chicken stock
2 tsp salt
1 tsp pepper

1 tsp dry basil
2 tsp dry oregano
1/2 tbsp hard goat cheese
3.5 oz. parmesan cheese, grated
1 tbsp fresh parsley leaves, minced

Directions

1. Place a large saucepan over medium heat. Heat in it the oil.
2. Cook in it the chicken with a pinch of salt for 4 min. Stir in the parsley, basil, tomato, and oregano.
3. Cook them until they become dry. Stir in the rice with stock.
4. Let them cook for 20 to 22 min until the risotto becomes creamy.
5. Once the time is up, stir in the parmesan and goat cheese. Serve your risotto warm.
6. Enjoy.

Risotto
Chicken Dinner

Prep Time: 10 mins
Total Time: 30 mins

Servings per Recipe: 3
Calories	458.1
Fat	16.5g
Cholesterol	59.5mg
Sodium	735.1mg
Carbohydrates	47.6g
Protein	29.0g

Ingredients

2 tbsp olive oil
10.5 oz. skinless chicken breasts, sliced into strips
1 large bell pepper, julienned
1/4 large red onion, julienned
1 tbsp white pepper
1 tbsp minced garlic paste
1 tbsp dried oregano
1 tbsp chopped fresh basil
1 tsp soy sauce

2 C. cooked rice
1/4 C. sliced black olives
1 C. chicken gravy
grated parmesan cheese
dried parsley
fresh parsley sprig

Directions

1. Place a large pan over medium heat. Heat in it the oil.
2. Cook in it the chicken strips for 3 min. Stir in the bell pepper, onion, pepper, garlic, and oregano.
3. Cook them for 3 min. Stir in the basil, soy sauce, rice, and black olives. Cook them for another 3 min.
4. Stir in the gravy and cook them until they start boiling. Lower the heat and let them cook for 9 to 11 min.
5. Stir in the parsley flakes with parmesan cheese. Serve your risotto warm.
6. Enjoy.

ROASTED
Mozzarella Risotto

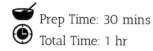

Prep Time: 30 mins
Total Time: 1 hr

Servings per Recipe: 10
Calories	386.5
Fat	18.8g
Cholesterol	94.0mg
Sodium	372.1mg
Carbohydrates	38.6g
Protein	16.4g

Ingredients

1.5 oz. butter
1 tbsp oil
1 large leek, sliced
1 garlic clove, crushed
2 C. Arborio rice
4 C. vegetable stock
1 C. water
1/2 C. cream
2 bunches asparagus, chopped
1.5 oz. baby spinach leaves

1 C. parmesan cheese, grated
2 tbsp parsley, chopped
2 eggs, lightly beaten
6.5 oz. baby bocconcini, drained
1/2 C. tasty cheese, grated

Directions

1. Place a large saucepan over medium heat. Heat in it the butter.
2. Cook in it the garlic with leek for 3 min. Stir in the rice and cook them for 2 min.
3. Stir in the water with cream and stock. Cook them until they start boiling.
4. Lower the heat and simmer it for 11 min.
5. Before you do anything, preheat the oven to 356 F.
6. Add the asparagus, spinach leaves, parmesan, and parsley.
7. Turn off the heat and add the eggs. Pour half of the mixture into a baking pan.
8. Top it with the bocconcini. Cover it with the remaining risotto. Top it with cheese.
9. Bake it for 26 min. Allow the risotto casserole to rest for 12 min. Serve it warm.
10. Enjoy.

Italian
Risotto

Prep Time: 15 mins
Total Time: 55 mins

Servings per Recipe: 4
Calories   760.1
Fat   17.3g
Cholesterol   15.2mg
Sodium   1017.3mg
Carbohydrates   128.1g
Protein   23.7g

Ingredients

4 C. vegetable broth
1 C. water
2 carrots, peeled and diced
12 stalks asparagus, trimmed and cut on the diagonal into lengths
2 bay leaves
2 tsp dried sage, divided
3 tbsp olive oil
1 large onion, chopped
1 lb. Arborio rice

1/2 C. limoncello, or chicken broth
2 C. fresh green peas
1/3 C. grated mozzarella cheese
1/4 C. grated parmesan cheese
salt and pepper

Directions

1. Place a large saucepan over medium heat. Stir in it the water with broth and heat them until they start boiling.
2. Stir in the carrots, asparagus, bay leaves, 1 tsp sage and salt and pepper.
3. Put on the lid and lower the heat. Let them cook for 12 min. Stain the veggies and place the broth aside.
4. Place a large pan over medium heat. Heat in it the oil. Cook in it the onion for 3 min.
5. Stir in the rice and cook them for 2 min. Stir in the limoncello and cook them for 1 min.
6. Stir 1 C. of broth and cook them until the rice absorbs it.
7. Repeat the process with the remaining broth until the rice absorbs all of it.
8. Turn off the heat and stir in the rest of the sage with veggies, green peas, and cheeses.
9. Cook them until the risotto becomes creamy. Serve it right away.
10. Enjoy.

25-MINUTE
Chicken Risotto

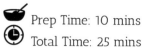 Prep Time: 10 mins

Total Time: 25 mins

Servings per Recipe: 4
Calories	342.9
Fat	5.6g
Cholesterol	79.4mg
Sodium	389.5mg
Carbohydrates	42.5g
Protein	28.4g

Ingredients

1/2 tbsp oil
1/2 onion, chopped
1 lb. ground chicken
1 (8 oz.) cans tomato sauce
1 C. long grain white rice, uncooked
1/4 C. parmesan cheese, grated

1/4-1/2 C. mozzarella cheese, shredded
salt and pepper

Directions

1. Prepare the rice by following the instructions on the package.
2. Place a large deep pan over medium heat. Heat in it the oil. Cook in it the onion for 3 min.
3. Stir in the meat with a pinch of salt and pepper. Cook them for 7 min. Discard the excess grease.
4. Stir in the tomato sauce and cook them for 2 min. Stir in the rice with cheeses.
5. Adjust the seasoning of your risotto then serve it warm.
6. Enjoy.

True Country Risotto

Prep Time: 45 mins
Total Time: 45 mins

Servings per Recipe: 6
Calories	459.0
Fat	14.5g
Cholesterol	52.5mg
Sodium	1059.2mg
Carbohydrates	58.2g
Protein	14.6g

Ingredients

2 quarts chicken broth
18 large shrimp, peeled and deveined
2 tbsp olive oil
4 tbsp unsalted butter
1 large onion, peeled and diced
2 C. Arborio rice

1 C. dry white wine
2 tbsp lemon zest
2 tbsp lemon juice
2 tbsp tarragon leaves, chopped

Directions

1. Place a large pot over medium heat. Heat in it the broth until it starts boiling.
2. Stir in the shrimp and cook them for 6 min. Drain it and place it aside.
3. Place a large saucepan over medium heat. Heat in it the oil with 2 tbsp of butter.
4. Cook in it the onion for 5 min. Stir in the wine and cook them until they start boiling.
5. Stir in the rice with 1 C. of boiling broth. Cook them while stirring until it is absorbed.
6. Repeat the process with the remaining broth until all of it is absorbed.
7. Add 1 tbsp of lemon juice, 1 tbsp of lemon zest, a pinch of salt and pepper. Cook them for 1 min.
8. Add the shrimp, tarragon and remaining 2 Tbsp butter. Serve your risotto warm.
9. Enjoy.

DIJON
Beef Risotto

Prep Time: 10 mins
Total Time: 25 mins

Servings per Recipe: 2
Calories	588.3
Fat	30.5g
Cholesterol	89.0mg
Sodium	557.7mg
Carbohydrates	47.4g
Protein	29.1g

Ingredients

8 oz. beef tenderloin steaks
1/4 C. kraft special collection sun-dried tomato vinaigrette dressing, Divided
3/4 C. zucchini, Chopped
1/4 C. carrot, Shredded
1/4 C. red pepper, Chopped

1 C. White Rice, Uncooked
3/4 C. chicken broth
1/2 C. milk
2 tbsp Grey Poupon Dijon Mustard

Directions

1. Place a large saucepan over medium heat. Heat in it 1 tbsp of dressing.
2. Cook in it the zucchini, carrot, and red pepper for 3 min.
3. Add the rice with broth, mustard, milk, a pinch of salt and pepper. Cook them until they start boiling.
4. Put on the lid and turn off the heat. Let it sit for 6 min.
5. Place a large pan over medium heat. Heat in it the rest of the dressing.
6. Cook in it the steaks for 5 to 6 min on each side. Serve them warm.
7. Enjoy.

Seattle
Vegetable Risotto

Prep Time: 10 mins
Total Time: 35 mins

Servings per Recipe: 6
Calories	777.8
Fat	36.0g
Cholesterol	94.1mg
Sodium	1688.3mg
Carbohydrates	89.9g
Protein	22.0g

Ingredients

10 C. chicken broth
1 1/2 lbs. small zucchini, chopped
10 oz. carrots, chopped
3/4 C. butter
3 C. Arborio rice
1/2 C. cream, scalded

3/4 C. grated parmesan cheese
2 tbsp minced parsley
1 tbsp minced basil

Directions

1. Place a large saucepan over medium heat. Heat in it the broth until it starts boiling.
2. Place a pot over medium heat. Stir in it the zucchini and carrots in ½ C. of butter. Cook them for 6 min.
3. Stir in 1 C. of stock. Cook them for 4 min while stirring until the rice absorbs it.
4. Repeat the process with the remaining broth until the rice absorbs all of it.
5. Once the time is up, add the rest of the butter with cream, a pinch of salt and pepper. Serve it warm.
6. Enjoy.

LATE OCTOBER
Pine Nut Risotto

Prep Time: 20 mins
Total Time: 1 hr

Servings per Recipe: 4
Calories   751.6
Fat   18.3g
Cholesterol   9.4mg
Sodium   138.5mg
Carbohydrates   129.3g
Protein   16.0g

Ingredients

2 tbsp olive oil
1 large onion, chopped
1 clove garlic, crushed
1 - 2 tbsp fresh sage
3 C. Arborio rice
2 C. fresh pumpkin, diced
1 3/4 pints boiling vegetable stock
1/3 C. pine nuts

1/3 C. shredded parmesan cheese
4 tbsp milk
1 pinch ground nutmeg
salt
ground black pepper

Directions

1. Place a large skillet over medium heat. Heat in it the oil.
2. Cook in it the sage with onion and sage for 6 min. Stir in the pumpkin with rice.
3. Cook them for 2 min. Stir 1/4 pint of stock. Cook them until the rice absorbs it while stirring.
4. Repeat the process with the remaining stock until the risotto becomes creamy.
5. Get a food processor: Combine in it the pine nuts, cheese, milk, and nutmeg. Blend them smooth.
6. Add it to the risotto with a pinch of salt and pepper. Cook them for 3 min then serve it warm.
7. Enjoy.

Oyster Mushroom and Barley Risotto (Brown Basmati Risotto)

Prep Time: 10 mins
Total Time: 1 hr 10 mins

Servings per Recipe: 4
Calories	194.3
Fat	3.8g
Cholesterol	5.5mg
Sodium	126.1mg
Carbohydrates	33.5g
Protein	9.5g

Ingredients

6 C. water
2/3 brown basmati rice
2/3 C. pearl barley
1 tsp olive oil
1 lb. oyster mushroom, sliced
1/2 C. vegetable broth

1/4 C. grated parmesan cheese
1/4 tsp ground pepper

Directions

1. Place a pot over medium heat. Heat in it the water until it starts boiling.
2. Stir in it the barley with rice and a pinch of salt. Bring them to a boil.
3. Lower the heat and let them cook for 46 min while stirring often.
4. Place a large skillet over medium heat. Heat in it the oil.
5. Cook in it the mushrooms for 9 min. Drain the rice and barley then add them to the pan.
6. Cook them for 2 min. Stir in the cheese with broth. Cook them until the risotto becomes creamy.
7. Adjust its seasoning then serve it warm.
8. Enjoy.

OVEN ROASTED
Risotto

Prep Time: 20 mins
Total Time: 1 hr 10 mins

Servings per Recipe: 6
Calories	391.6
Fat	23.9g
Cholesterol	42.3mg
Sodium	620.4mg
Carbohydrates	37.2g
Protein	8.3g

Ingredients

4 tbsp butter
1 onion, chopped
1 tbsp minced garlic
2 celery ribs, diced
1 small green bell pepper, seeded and
chopped
1 (10 oz.) can cream of mushroom
soup, undiluted
5 oz. milk
1 (10 oz.) cans sliced mushrooms, well

drained, sliced and sautéed
1/2 C. mayonnaise
1/2 C. sour cream
black pepper
1/2 tsp garlic powder
2 1/2 C. cold cooked rice
1/3 C. grated parmesan cheese

Directions

1. Before you do anything, preheat the oven to 350 F.
2. Grease a baking dish with some butter. Place it aside.
3. Place a large pan over medium heat. Heat in it the butter. Cook in it the onion with bell pepper and celery for 6 min.
4. Stir in the garlic and cook them for 3 min. Drain the mixture and place it in a large bowl.
5. Stir the soup, milk, drained canned mushrooms mayonnaise, sour cream, black pepper, garlic powder and cooked cold rice.
6. Season them with a pinch of salt and pepper. Combine them well. Spoon the mixture into the greased casserole.
7. Top it with cheese then bake it for 36 to 46 min. Serve it warm.
8. Enjoy.